Stay Healthy!

What should we eat?

Angela Royston

www.raintreepublishers.co.uk
Visit our website to find out more information about **Raintree** books.

To order:
☎ Phone 44 (0) 1865 888112
🖹 Send a fax to 44 (0) 1865 314091
💻 Visit the Raintree Bookshop at **www.raintreepublishers.co.uk** to browse our catalogue and order online.

First published in Great Britain by Raintree, Halley Court, Jordan Hill, Oxford OX2 8EJ, part of Harcourt Education.
Raintree is a registered trademark of Harcourt Education Ltd.

© Harcourt Education Ltd 2006
The moral right of the proprietor has been asserted.

Editorial: Jilly Attwood
Design: Jo Hinton-Malivoire, bigtop
Picture Research: Ruth Blair, Ginny Stroud-Lewis
Production: Severine Ribierre
Originated by Modern Age
Printed and bound in China by South China Printing Company

ISBN 1 406 20047 6
10 09 08 07 06
10 9 8 7 6 5 4 3 2 1

British Library Cataloguing in Publication Data
Royston, Angela
What should we eat?. - (Stay healthy!)
613.2
A full catalogue record for this book is available from the British Library.

Acknowledgements
The publishers would like to thank the following for permission to reproduce photographs:
Alamy Images p4.(Banana Stock), 12 & 23c; Getty Images p.8 & 23b(Taxi); Harcourt Education pp.6, 10, 16, 19, 21(Gareth Boden), p.20 & 23a(Liz Eddison), pp.7, 9, 11, 13, 14, 15, 17, 22, 23d(Tudor Photography); photolibrary.com p.18; Science Photo Library p.5(Maximilian Stock Ltd).

Cover photograph of a person holding an apple reproduced with permission of Alamy. Back cover images reproduced with permission of Alamy Images (Banana Stock) and Harcourt Education (Tudor Photography).

Every effort has been made to contact copyright holders of any material reproduced in this book. Any omissions will be rectified in subsequent printings if notice is given to the publishers.

Our thanks to Dr Sarah Schenker, Dietitian, for her help in the preparation of this book.

The paper used to print this book comes from sustainable resources.

Some words are shown in bold, **like this**. You can find them in the picture glossary on page 23.

Contents

Are some foods better than others?

Your body needs many kinds of foods.

Some kinds of food are good for you, like these grapes.

But you should not eat too many
of these snacks.

Which foods should you eat most of?

You should eat mostly vegetables, and food like rice.

Rice has lots of **starch**.

Cereal is starchy, too.

Why do you think starchy food is good for you?

Starchy food gives you **energy**.

You need energy to jump.

bread

rice

pasta

These foods are starchy, too.

You should eat some starchy
food at every meal.

Should you eat fruit and vegetables?

Fruit and vegetables are good for you!

You should eat many different kinds of fruit and vegetables.

How many different kinds should you eat every day?

Count them in the picture!

Do you need to eat meat?

Meat has **protein** in it.

Your body needs protein to grow.

You should eat some protein every day.

tuna fish

egg

beans

cheese

These foods have protein, too.

You do not have to eat meat to get protein.

Why is too much fat bad for you?

nut

You need to eat some fat.

But too much fat is bad for your heart.

ice-cream

banana

salami

Which of these snacks do you think has the least fat?

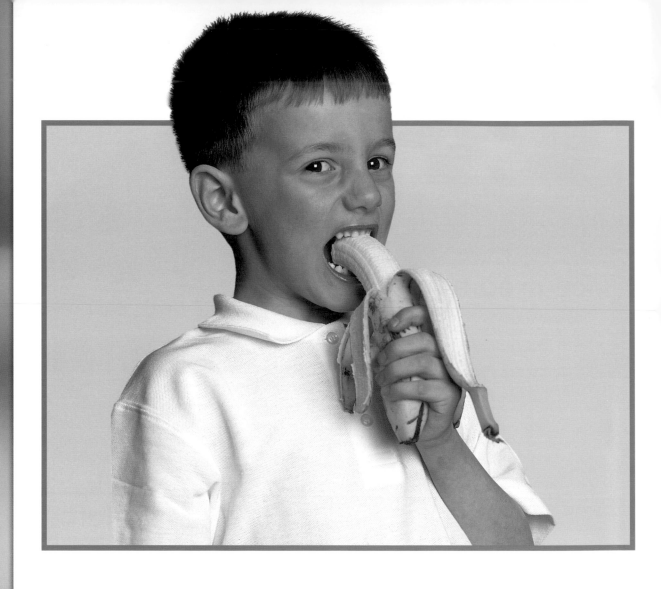

The banana has the least fat!

Are all snacks fatty?

These snacks have very little fat.

It is good to eat low fat snacks.

Why is too much sugar bad for you?

Sweet foods are tasty.

But you should have them only as treats.

Sweet foods and drinks are sugary.

Too much sugar is bad for
your teeth.

What is a food allergy?

Some people are **allergic** to nuts or other foods.

They get ill if they eat these foods.

They have to make sure they do not eat these foods.

They have to check the labels on food packets.

Make a healthy sandwich!

1. Spread two slices of bread with butter or margarine.

2. Cover one piece of bread with slices of cheese, tomatoes, cucumber, and lettuce.

3. Place the second slice of bread on top.

4. Enjoy eating your healthy cheese sandwich!

Glossary

 **allergic** when something that is not usually unhealthy makes you ill

 **energy** what you need to move or do anything

 **protein** kind of food that helps you to grow

 **starch** food that gives you energy

Index

Note to parents and teachers

Reading non-fiction texts for information is an important part of a child's literacy development. Readers can be encouraged to ask simple questions and then use the text to find the answers. Most chapters in this book begin with a question. Read the questions together. Look at the pictures. Talk about what the answer might be. Then read the text to find out if your predictions were correct. To develop readers' enquiry skills, encourage them to think of other questions they might ask about the topic. Discuss where you could find the answers. Assist children in using the contents page, picture glossary and index to practise research skills and new vocabulary.